Praise for *Top 10 Kicks*

Kicking is an important part of training in many martial arts, which is why you should read *Top 10 Kicks Every Fighter Should Know* by Augustus John Roe. This book is full of helpful tips and tricks and useful for practitioners of any style. I especially enjoyed the thought-provoking ratings he generated for each kick, scoring each for damage, speed, and difficulty. Even though I have been training for nearly 40 years, I still found little things here and there that deepened my understanding of kicking, things that I am excited to pass on to my students and use against my opponents!

—**Joe Varady**, Grandmaster 7th dan, author of *The Art and Science Training Series* (*Stick, Staff, Sword, and Self-Defense*)

A comprehensive and accessible guide to martial arts kicking; it makes it easy to put into practice for fighters of any level and practitioners of any martial art. Roe provides scaling for multiple components of martial arts, such as damage, difficulty, and speed, along with tips to enhance training and execution. I highly recommend *Top 10 Kicks Every Fighter Should Know* for anyone who wants to improve their kicking game.

—**Kamil Nguyen Van**, Lightweight MMA Champion (Lion Championship, VMMAF)

Top 10 Kicks Every Fighter Should Know is an outstanding page turner. Augustus John Roe does an expert job of describing the best used kicks for self-defense. He points out the beauty and athleticism of kicks but advises correctly how the simplest ones are usually the best.

I really liked how he provided various set up techniques along with great ways to practice each kick for improvement. I will be using all his recommendations.

I found myself looking forward to the unusual "angles" chapter. I thought including a kick from the ground was a very smart idea. I look forward to having all my students read this book as it is written well and accurate.

—**Sensei Jim Pawlak** 6th dan Shotokan Karate, owner of Fair Haven Martial Arts, NJ.

Since the earliest days of martial arts, the kick has been a dominant technique. In *Top 10 Kicks Every Fighter Should Know*, Augustus John Roe effectively pays homage to these powerful moves. This well-thought-out book is an enjoyable read, especially with its engaging success stories involving the kicks.

The variety of kicks presented provides readers with numerous combative options. The top ten kicks are drawn from various martial arts and sports, which I particularly appreciate given my eclectic martial arts background. Every martial art has its own strengths, including its kicking techniques. I especially liked how the author clearly classified each kick based on damage, speed, and difficulty.

This book concisely educates martial artists of all levels, from beginners to advanced practitioners. I highly recommend *Top 10 Kicks* to anyone looking to add a real kick to their martial arts practice!

—**Andrew Zerling**, martial artist, award winning author of *Sumo for Mixed Martial Arts*

Augustus John Roe's compendium of leg techniques stuns the reader both in its concision and depth. With its intuitive array of diagrams and illustrations, *Top 10 Kicks Every Fighter Should Know* comprises an indispensable entry to kicking for the martial arts enthusiast.

—**Thầy Quảng Huyền** or Master Quảng Huyền

This book is a fantastic resource for any martial artist looking to expand their kicking arsenal, as well as beginners who want to learn the basics. Roe's clear and concise explanations, coupled with practical demonstrations, make the techniques accessible. I really enjoyed the anecdotes from the author, who described real situations where he and others have used the techniques. This book is a must-have for anyone serious about improving their kicking game. Highly recommended!

—**Sensei Clement Martin**, head instructor
Kishinkai Aikido, Vietnam

Top 10 Kicks Every Fighter Should Know is one of the most solid breakdowns of practical kicking I've seen in a long time. Augustus Roe manages to keep things simple without watering anything down. Whether you're a striker, someone training for real-world situations, or just trying to build a strong base as a martial artist, this book delivers.

Each kick is explained with real-world application in mind—not just for sport, but for actual survival and self-defense scenarios too. I appreciated the focus on fundamentals over flashy techniques. The setups, drills, and tips are easy to follow but deep enough for any level to sharpen their skills. As someone who trains and teaches both modern and historical martial arts—from MMA to tactical defense and sword work—I think this book deserves a spot in every fighter's library. It's not just about the kicks; it's about the mindset behind them too.

—**Patrick Chitwood**, martial artist, founder of the Warriors Tribe brand, creator of The Tribal Warrior publishing company

TOP 10 KICKS
EVERY FIGHTER SHOULD KNOW

AUGUSTUS JOHN ROE

YMAA Publication Center
Wolfeboro, NH USA

YMAA Publication Center, Inc.
PO Box 480
Wolfeboro, New Hampshire 03894
1-800-669-8892 • info@ymaa.com • www.ymaa.com
ISBN: 9781594393686 (print) • ISBN: 9781594393693 (ebook)

Copyright ©2025 by Augustus John Roe
All rights reserved including the right of reproduction in whole or in part in any form. Any use of this intellectual property for text and data mining or computational analysis including as training material for artificial intelligence systems is strictly prohibited without express written consent. For permission requests, contact the Publisher.

Edited by Doran Hunter
Cover design by Axie Breen
This book is typeset in Adobe Garamond and Source Sans.
Photos and illlustrations provided by author.

20250828

Publisher's Cataloging in Publication

Names: Roe, Augustus John, author.
Title: Top 10 kicks every fighter should know / Augustus John Roe.
Other titles: Top ten kicks every fighter should know
Description: Wolfeboro, NH USA : YMAA Publication Center, Inc., [2025]
Identifiers: LCCN: 2025942768 | ISBN: 9781594393686 (print) | 9781594393693 (ebook)
Subjects: LCSH: Martial arts--Kicking--Handbooks, manuals, etc. | Martial arts--Handbooks, manuals, etc. | Karate--Kicking--Handbooks, manuals, etc. | Kickboxing--Handbooks, manuals, etc. | Tae kwon do--Kicking--Handbooks, manuals, etc. | Self-defense--Kicking--Handbooks, manuals, etc. | LCGFT: Self-instructional works. | BISAC: SPORTS & RECREATION / Martial Arts / General | SPORTS & RECREATION / Training | SPORTS & RECREATION / Health & Safety.
Classification: LCC: GV1102.7.K52 R64 2025 | DDC: 796.8--dc23

Disclaimer:
The authors and publisher of the material are NOT RESPONSIBLE in any manner whatsoever for any injury which may occur through reading or following the instructions in this manual.

The activities physical or otherwise, described in this manual may be too strenuous or dangerous for some people.

Warning: While self-defense is legal, fighting is illegal. If you don't know the difference you'll go to jail because you aren't defending yourself. Readers are encouraged to be aware of all appropriate local and national laws relating to self-defense, reasonable force, and act in accordance with all applicable laws at all times. Neither the author nor the publisher assumes any responsibility for the use or misuse of information contained in this book.

Nothing in this document constitutes a legal opinion nor should any of its contents be treated as such. While the author believes that everything herein is accurate, any questions regarding specific self-defense situations, legal liability, and/or interpretation of federal, state, or local laws should always be addressed by an attorney at law.

Printed in USA.

CONTENTS

Introduction	v
Damage, Speed, and Difficulty Descriptors	viii
Notes on Safety and Flexibility	x
Notes on the Writing	xi
Straight Kicks	**1**
Front Snap Kick	3
Procedure	4
Possible Setup	8
Kicking Tips	11
Front Push Kick	12
Procedure	13
Possible Setup	17
Kicking Tips	19
Success Story	20
Side Kick	22
Procedure	23
Possible Setup	27
Kicking Tips	30
Back Kick	31
Procedure	32
Possible Setup	36
Kicking Tips	39
Success Story	39

Circular Kicks — 41

Roundhouse Snap Kick — 42
   Procedure — 43
   Possible Setup — 47
   Kicking Tips — 50
   Success Story — 50

Roundhouse Slam Kick — 52
   Procedure — 53
   Possible Setup — 57
   Kicking Tips — 60

Hook Kick — 61
   Procedure — 62
   Possible Setup — 66
   Kicking Tips: — 69
   Success Story — 69

Unusual-Angle Kicks — 71

Question Mark Kick — 72
   Procedure — 73
   Possible Setup — 77
   Kicking Tips — 80

Oblique Kick — 81
   Procedure — 82
   Possible Setup — 86
   Kicking Tips — 89
   Success Story — 89

Up Kick — 91
   Procedure — 92
   Possible Setup — 96
   Kicking Tips — 99

Afterword — 101
Glossary of Terms — 105
About the Author — 107

INTRODUCTION

While punching might be the most widely used combat technique, it is certainly not the be-all and end-all of fighting. As a traditional martial arts instructor, combat sport fighter, and kung fu movie aficionado, I, like many others, have always found there to be something special about the skill, speed, and sheer power of a good kick.

Although detractors may consider kicking to be too challenging to learn or too risky to perform in real-life scenarios, this could not be further from the truth.

Kicks *do* typically require far more practice and perseverance to master than punches or even simple throws. However, when used correctly, they are more than just another string on the fighter's bow. Instead they provide an extra layer of depth and complexity to one's combat skills.

Besides being naturally powerful techniques, kicks can also be used tactically in a wide variety of situations, such as to control range, surprise opponents, or set up further strikes. Meanwhile, the training required for kicking provides improved strength, fitness, balance, and flexibility by utilizing the entire body in a holistic way. Kicks are also aesthetically pleasing, looking awesome to spectators and feeling even better to perform!

As I'm sure you can tell, I am a strong advocate of kicking. However, I am also of the school of thought that believes simple techniques performed well are almost always better than more complex ones.

Therefore, this book has been written with functionality in mind, focusing on fundamental kicking skills for beginner and intermediate fighters. Even though there are not many spinning or jumping techniques in these pages, experienced practitioners may still find valuable kicking variations, drills, or approaches to add to their repertoire.

This book features ten of the most practical and effective kicks, drawn from both my own and various contributors' experiences. Whether your goals are fitness and flexibility, training for competition, or simply to enhance your combat skills, the kicks included in these pages will serve you well.

All the techniques in this book begin from an orthodox stance (left foot forward). This stance is prevalent in combat sports as it allows right-handed fighters to control distance and set up combinations with their left hand or foot before delivering power techniques from the right. If you're a southpaw fighter (right foot forward), simply mirror the positions shown. Keep in mind that proficient fighters can use both orthodox and southpaw stances, so once you've mastered these kicks in your natural stance, practice them from the opposite position too.

It should also be noted that while the kicks in this book are broken down step by step, as you become more proficient at kicking, these steps will flow together to become a single seamless movement. However, practicing them slowly at first in isolated movements allows you to develop proper technique before building up to full speed.

While it is not crucial that readers master every single kick in this book, a core of at least five solid kicks should be sufficient to allow most fighters the variation they need to succeed in most situations.

It should also be noted that in real self-defense situations, fighters should never attempt high kicks, as they significantly increase the risk of losing balance and falling—a potentially dangerous outcome. As a result, the "Setups" in this book focus exclusively on low targets, making them safer and easier to perform. However, in martial arts training and combat sports, these Setups can be adapted for higher targets. Beyond scoring points or improving flexibility, the rationale is that if you can kick effectively at a high target, kicking at a low target will be even easier and more powerful!

A typical left-leg-forward fighting stance

Each entry in this book will follow a consistent format, as detailed below:
- Name: most widely used/recognized name of kick
- Introduction: an overview, summary of the kick's function and a description of how it generates power, and how it should feel when performed correctly, referred to throughout as "character"

- Striking Surface: which part of the foot/leg is used
- Targets: where the kick is designed to land
- Common in: styles in which the kick is typically found
- Damage, Speed, and Difficulty: each rated 1 to 5
- Success Story: in some entries
- Procedure: step-by-step instructions and photos
- Possible Setup: suggested method for delivering the kick
- Kicking Tips: how to avoid common mistakes or perform the kick better
- Training Exercise: suggested ways to practice the kick

Damage, Speed, and Difficulty Descriptors

Each technique is rated on a scale of 1 to 5 based on three traits: damage, speed, and difficulty. These ratings are subjective, meaning that some practitioners may find certain techniques easier, faster, or more powerful than others. Therefore, these ratings should be considered a teaching aid rather than a definitive classification.

A perfect score (5) in all areas is unrealistic since damage, speed, and difficulty do not operate independently. For example, a technique that scores a 5 in speed is unlikely to also score a 5 in damage.

Each entry will be marked with a number of symbols representing these criteria, as shown below.

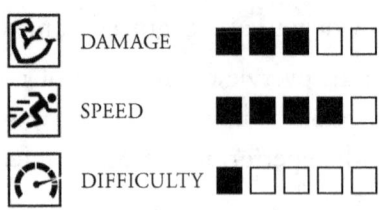

The descriptors for each of these areas are displayed in the following chart:

DAMAGE

1	**Minimal**	Primarily used for scoring points in competition or as a setup for other techniques.
2	**Light**	Inflicts some pain but is generally better used as part of a combination or to create an opening.
3	**Significant**	Causes temporary damage but is unlikely to end a fight on its own.
4	**Heavy**	May cause significant, potentially long-lasting damage, and can end a fight if executed cleanly.
5	**Critical**	Can cause permanent damage or death. Guaranteed to end an altercation if used effectively with full force.

SPEED

1	**Very Slow**	Easy to see coming. Must be set up well or disguised to be successful.
2	**Somewhat Slow**	Can be effective when obscured or used against an unsuspecting opponent.
3	**Reasonable**	Can generally be delivered with enough speed to be successful.
4	**Fast**	Moves quickly enough to succeed the majority of the time when delivered properly.
5	**Extremely Rapid**	Executed with very high speed when delivered well.

DIFFICULTY

1	**Advanced**	Highly specialized and technically challenging. Requires extensive practice but is likely to be effective when executed well.
2	**Difficult**	Hard to perform and requires significant practice to be effective in combat.
3	**Intermediate**	Relatively simple to perform but requires training and practice for combat effectiveness.
4	**Fairly Easy**	Utilizes mostly natural movements and requires minimal practice to be effective.
5	**Easy**	Simple and intuitive, using natural body mechanics, and can be performed by individuals with no prior training.

Notes on Safety and Flexibility

Before starting to kick, you must ensure that you are in a suitable environment. This means you should be on stable ground with decent levels of grip. It should be relatively soft (i.e., not concrete or stone tiles) and clear of obstructions. If you are lacking space, it is recommended that you kick slowly, focusing on accuracy and technique rather than speed or power.

When working with training partners, always ensure you are equally cautious. Focus on your target, making sure not to kick too low or too high, and remember that it is easy to slip or slide past a pad or punching bag, especially when sweaty. Also, be wary of the potential damage that could be caused by kicking a training partner too hard, even if they are holding a pad or wearing protection.

You MUST also ensure that you are warmed up before kicking (or any workout) so as not to risk injury.

It is also recommended that all readers intending to practice kicking develop flexibility by stretching at least two to three times a week as part of a kicking routine. Ideal stretching should include a combination of "dynamic," "static," and "PNF" (proprioceptive neuromuscular facilitation) stretching. PNF stretching is also known as "contract-relax" stretching.

Dynamic stretching involves moving the muscles in a similar way to how they are used to kick, but without the additional muscular strength involved in striking. Examples include standing leg raises and alternating toe touches. This is probably the most important step in warming up and will prevent injury.

Static stretching is what one typically pictures when thinking of stretching and involves holding positions for an extended period, usually ten to thirty seconds. For example, placing the heel on a table and reaching forward toward the toes.

PNF stretching is useful for increasing flexibility and involves extending the muscle to its maximum (or near maximum) in a static position and then contracting the muscle to extend the stretch. An example is placing your foot up on a table then tensing the leg to push down against the surface for several seconds before relaxing and repeating.

Finally, it is important to recognize your limits and not overexert yourself when stretching or kicking. Always start off slowly and err on the side of caution. Feeling some discomfort when developing flexibility is normal. Pain is not. If a body part hurts, stop what you are doing immediately and follow the RICE principle (rest, ice, compression, elevation) to allow yourself to fully recover before restarting your training.

Notes on the Writing

It should be noted that the names of the techniques are often interchangeable depending on the practitioner's background. For example, muay thai fighters may refer to a "roundhouse kick" as a "side kick." As a result, please keep this in consideration when conducting further research.

Additionally, when writing this book, I tried to come up with an encompassing word to refer to the way the kick looks and performs as well as to the internal sensation for the kicker. For example, "like a spear-thrust" or "with a hammering quality." But finding no perfectly suitable term in English, I have chosen the word "character" to refer to what could be considered as "style," "flavor," or "sensation."

Rather than repeating the phrases "martial arts" and "combat sports" to refer to traditional fighting styles and modern sporting versions, respectively, I have elected to use the term "martial arts" throughout the remainder of the book to refer to both.

Any uncommon or martial-arts-specific words (e.g., "jab" or "chamber") have been included in a glossary of terms at the end of the book. Please refer to it if there is any confusion.

CHAPTER ONE

Straight Kicks

In the realm of martial arts, many fighters consider attacking with straight techniques to be the most intuitive and accessible method. After all, the fastest journey between any two points is always a straight line.

Straight kicks are among the safest to perform as they do not require the fighter to develop power using large swinging motions like circular kicks or require shifts of balance as is sometimes the case with those thrown from unusual angles.

Despite relying on natural motions, using straight kicks effectively requires a certain amount of finesse and attention to detail that can often be skipped over with more powerful and less direct techniques.

In addition, the straight kicks featured in this chapter are not all performed with the same "character." They may snap, push, or even crush. However, once fighters understand the subtleties of using different straight kicks, they can become some of the fastest and most powerful techniques in their arsenal.

This chapter will look at the fundamental three types of straight kicks: front, side, and back kicks.

Front Snap Kick

The front snap kick uses the ball of the foot, thrown in a rapid whipping or snapping motion toward targets on the center line of the opponent.

It is a precision technique rather than a power strike. However, its speed and accuracy make it a formidable attack. When thrown from the rear leg, it can serve as a defensive strike while still packing enough force to deliver a knockout blow.

Power is developed from an upward thrust of the hips, which lifts the body onto the ball of the standing foot. This is emphasized by a rapid snapping motion that comes from extending the knee to carry momentum through.

Character: This kick is like a cracking whip. It should shoot up fast, biting and stinging the opponent, and return with similar speed. When performed this way, it can easily deliver enough force to end a fight.

Striking Surface: Typically, the ball of the foot or the heel at closer range. The heel will deliver more pushing force, but striking with the ball of the foot will lend the kick more whipping power.

Targets: Face, chin, throat, chest, abdomen, groin.

Common in: Karate, taekwondo, MMA.

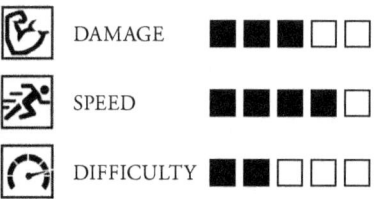

DAMAGE ■■■□□
SPEED ■■■■□
DIFFICULTY ■■□□□

Procedure

1. From a typical fighting stance, straighten your hips and square up by stepping slightly outward with the lead foot.

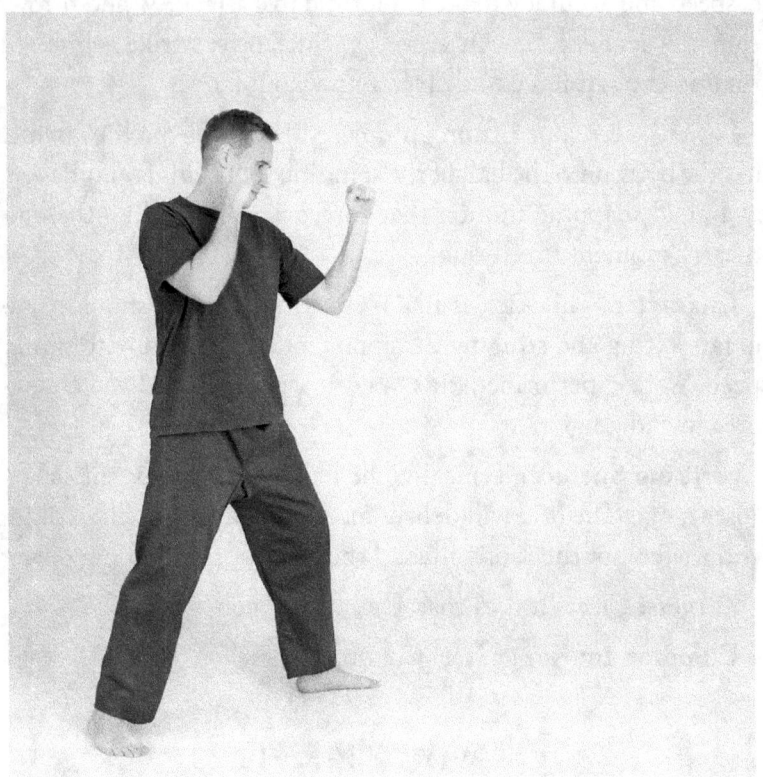

2. Step up with the rear leg, pivoting the toes on the standing foot outward at approximately 45-degrees. Meanwhile, pull up the toes on your kicking foot and aim your knee toward your target.

3. Whip your foot forward, following the trajectory of your knee and extending the hip and ball of the foot fully (or the heel in close range).

4. Re-chamber the knee, quickly returning to complete the whipping motion. Then step back down into the foot's original position at the rear of the stance.

Possible Setup

1. Throw a jab (a fast punch) with the lead hand then a cross (power punch) with the rear hand before pulling them back to a guard to cover your face.

2. Throw another jab, making your opponent recoil or step back expecting you to follow with a second cross.

3. Instead of punching, immediately launch the rear leg up into a front snap kick toward the groin or abdomen.

Kicking Tips
- Ensure the chamber is lifted high (at least to chest height). This will make it harder for the kick to be blocked and easier for the ball of the foot to penetrate through gaps in the opponent's guard.
- Pull back the toes to strike with the ball of the foot. This will avoid damaging the toes and ensure that the power of the kick is focused into a small surface area.
- Ensure there is a slight bend in the standing leg and keep the head and body mostly upright rather than leaning too far backward as this will reduce balance.

Training Exercise: Tennis Ball Kicks for Accuracy
1. Pierce a hole through either end of a tennis ball and tie a string through it. Hang the ball from the ceiling (or something overhead).
2. Start slow and low, working on precision with the ball of the foot, delivering an accurate front snap kick, and ensuring your chamber is correctly positioned.
3. Once you can hit the target accurately at least three to five times consecutively with each leg, start to increase the speed, or practice kicking at the ball when it is in motion.
4. Make the task more challenging by changing ranges. Kick from a closer range using the heel or raise the target higher until it is at head height or above.

Front Push Kick

Commonly known in muay thai and MMA as a "teep," the front push kick is a straight attack that thrusts forward from the body on a horizontal plane to launch the opponent backward. While it can be performed from the lead leg, using an almost identical procedure as the one that follows, it is most effective when thrown from the rear due to the body weight following through. Therefore, many muay thai fighters will simply add a quick switch with the feet to change stance before kicking.

The front push kick is often used tactically rather than as a direct knockout technique. It can create space for other strikes or keep an advancing opponent away. This also makes it ideal for self-defense scenarios where badly injuring an opponent might be unnecessary. However, it should be noted that the kick can cause significant injury by launching the opponent backward into obstacles or onto the floor.

The power of this kick comes from a thrust of the hip muscles and horizontal extension of the leg, which uses the quads, glutes, and abs in unison with a small slide forward to project its velocity through the target.

Character: While the front snap kick acts like a whip or spear, utilizing a stabbing motion, the front push kick is like a battering ram at speed or a barge pole when used more tactically.

Striking Surface: The ball of the foot or flat foot.

Targets: Face, chest, solar plexus, lead hip.

Common in: Muay thai, Khmer boxing, kickboxing, MMA, self-defense systems.

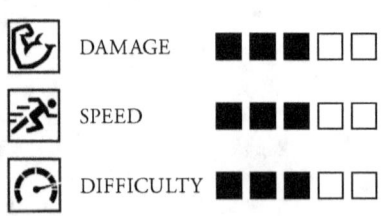

Procedure

1. From a typical fighting stance, step the lead foot out at approximately 45 degrees into an almost-square position and shift the weight slightly forward.

2. Rise up onto your lead leg, bringing your rear knee to chest height in a chamber, keeping it close to the body, and the toes pulled up.

3. Pivot slightly on the standing foot as you thrust from the hips, extending the ball of the kicking foot. Add a slight backward lean and throw the lead arm down past the leg as the rear hand protects your face.

4. Pull the foot sharply back to the chamber position to prevent it being grabbed. Step back into a defensive position, or step down in front and continue to advance.

Possible Setup

1. Throw a low slamming roundhouse (see "Circular Kicks 2") once or twice with the rear leg, before backing off.

2. Wait for the opponent to recover, then fake another low kick. As the opponent moves back to defend, or goes to block the kick, quickly raise the knee.

STRAIGHT KICKS 19

3. Deliver the front push kick to the chest or face, sending them flying backward.

Kicking Tips
- Focus on extending the ball of the foot, ensuring it strikes the surface first. Follow through by extending your hip fully and swinging the lead arm downward.
- Slide forward or even jump slightly on the ball of the foot to increase momentum.

- Try to focus on an explosion outward from the hips. The greater the speed of the horizontal thrust, the more force will be generated.

Training Exercise: Power thrusts with a partner for technique and strength.
1. Ensure you are training in a space with a soft floor (on mats, carpet, or grass) and work with a partner holding a pad. Have the partner take a wide stance, bracing the pad against their side or shoulder like a shield.
2. Start with your back to a wall and the partner within close kicking range, meaning you will have to use a tight chamber and thrust to create space.
3. Try to push your partner backward with each subsequent kick while they brace and try to resist. Change legs each time.
4. Push them all the way to the far side of the room. Then swap roles. See who can move the partner furthest with the least number of kicks.

Success Story

A friend of mine was once walking outside a city center shopping mall with his girlfriend at his side. Being a gentleman, he was carrying the heavy shopping bags, one in each hand.

It was dusk, and the light was fading fast. From across the sidewalk, a strange-looking woman started approaching them quickly. The odd woman was shouting erratically, obviously distressed about something, making a beeline for his girlfriend, possibly with malicious intent.

With both of his hands engaged and a potential threat fast approaching, my friend had to make a split-second decision. Fortunately, his martial arts training kicked in and before the crazed woman got within range of grabbing (or who knows what else) his girlfriend, he raised his knee and thrust outward, catching the much-smaller woman smoothly with a light, but well-placed front push kick to the chest.

The kick was controlled enough that it didn't send the stranger flying but put some distance between them, allowing my friend time to reevaluate the situation. Fortunately, in this case, the kick dissuaded what he could now see was a clearly mentally ill woman from approaching again, and they were able to simply walk away, no harm done.

While I'm not recommending people start push kicking away everyone that approaches them, this is an excellent example of scalable force. The kick was adapted to be suitable for a situation and demonstrates how it can be used effectively without causing significant injury.

Side Kick

This kick is typically thrown from a high chamber using the lead leg, which shoots out perpendicular to the chest with the heel or blade of the foot extended. The weight remains on the rear leg throughout.

It is often used like a jab in combination with punches, both offensively and defensively. Ideally, the kick lands below the opponent's guard, sneaking into the abdomen, floating ribs, or even the thigh or knee to stop them advancing. If the kicker is extremely flexible, it can also be used toward the face; however, the length of the foot when turned sideways makes this easier to block. Side kicks are often effective when used against kickboxing and MMA fighters as they are absent in many ring sports.

The power of the kick comes from the sideways extension of the hip, relying on the glutes, quads, and hip flexors to generate force. While the side kick can be thrown from the rear leg, the additional time it takes to bring the chamber across slows it significantly, reducing functionality.

Character: The kick is a fast and sharp attack that plunges through a narrow point of contact, like a straight sword thrust. It is not usually intended to knock out or destroy (at least not without the use of an additional step-through or jump to increase power). Instead, it works tactically, creating or maintaining distance or as part of a flurry of strikes.

Striking Surface: The blade of the foot or the heel, the former for greater precision and the latter for greater force.

Targets: Knee, thigh, abdomen, chest, throat, face.

Common in: Karate, taekwondo, kung fu, savate, jeet kune do.

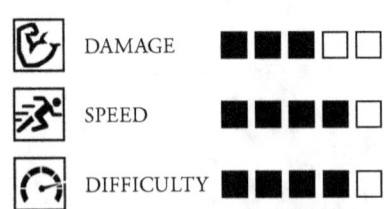

Procedure

1. Keeping your weight on the rear leg, step the lead foot slightly across the body and enough so your heel is almost lined up with the target. Do not step any further or it will make your intentions easy to read.

2. Raise the lead knee to chest height, with the toes pulled up while pivoting the standing foot 180-degrees from the target. Your rear heel, hips, shoulders, and lead heel are now all on a parallel plane.

3. Execute a linear thrust sending the heel or blade of the lead foot across a straight plane, while extending the back to provide more thrust.

4. Pull the kicking leg back to the chamber immediately to prevent it from being caught, then step down without throwing your weight forward and opening yourself to attack.

Possible Setup

1. Fire off a jab toward the face, making your opponent back up and giving you space to kick.

2. Throw a second jab and slide off angle toward the opponent's front side at 45 degrees, staying out of range. Your opponent will want to turn to square up and open their front side to attack.

3. As the opponent adjusts, raise your lead leg and thrust it outward into the abdomen, floating ribs, or knee.

Kicking Tips

- Focus on thrusting out the foot on as horizontal a plane as possible. Straighten the leg fully on the kick, aligning the heel, hip, and shoulder on the kicking side with the toes angled slightly downward toward the ground.
- Ensure that you turn the rear foot fully 180 degrees when you strike; otherwise, you are likely to be off balance.
- Slide slightly forward (or backward when used defensively) on your standing leg as you kick. This momentum will lend your side kick additional power.

Training Exercise: Speed kicks to work on closing/creating range.

1. Work with a partner. They will hold a soft stick (e.g., a pool noodle, striking paddle, or stick with a boxing glove on the end) in one hand and a pad in the other.
2. From just out of kicking range, you must slide in, stab a side kick into the pad, and start to retreat.
3. As soon as you make contact, your partner will bring the stick down from overhead toward you. You must slide back out of range before the strike lands.
4. Alternate between legs and doing this head on and at 45-degree angles to your partner's inside and outside space.

Back Kick

This is an extremely fast and powerful technique, generally considered one of the most devastating kicks in all of martial arts. It involves lifting the leg up straight from the ground while turning away and thrusting the heel out behind you. Because the kick chambers facing away from the opponent, it is difficult to see and thus difficult to block.

The back kick can be used defensively by spinning away from the opponent with the lead leg to act as both a dodge and concurrent attack. However, many fighters would argue it is best applied offensively when moving quickly toward the opponent. Due to the backward extension of the hip, it usually cannot be used at height and is primarily a midsection strike, but it is extremely dangerous nonetheless.

Power comes from several large muscle groups, including the back, thighs, and glutes, used in a natural extension. This, coupled with the momentum and centrifugal force of the spin, generates devastating power.

Character: This kick should have a slamming feeling, much like the motion of swinging a sledgehammer or a battering ram driving through a door.

Striking Surface: The heel should lead the kick. Using any other part of the foot will reduce power.

Targets: Groin, abdomen, chest, floating ribs.

Common in: MMA, kickboxing, karate, taekwondo, kung fu, self-defense systems.

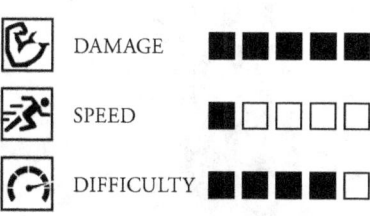

Procedure

1. Step your rear leg forward across your body at approximately 45 degrees, then turn your head and torso, bringing them to the front, looking over what is now your lead shoulder.

2. Raise the rear leg, chambering the heel up beside your lead thigh, with your knee close to your abdomen and your toes pulled up. Keep your rear hand up by your face and your lead hand out in front.

3. Lean away from the target, extending your kicking leg out directly beneath your body, leading with the heel, until you reach the target. Extend the same arm but keep your rear fist close to your face to help maintain balance.

4. Turn your body to the front, re-chambering the leg, and step down in front to continue pushing forward, completing the spin.

Possible Setup

1. Throw a cross while stepping through with the rear leg. Most opponents will back up out of range of the cross.

2. As your punch reaches its maximum range, continue to turn on the balls of your feet until you are looking over your now lead shoulder and throw a backfist toward the opponent's face.

3. As they block or move out of the way, lift the rear leg and throw your back kick into the opponent's abdomen or ribs.

Kicking Tips
- Keep the shoulder you are looking over shrugged to protect your face from incoming punches.
- Ensure you keep your head and torso upright as you turn. This will enable you to do so faster and ensure you do not fall forward when you strike.
- Turn your head fully, focusing on the target with your eyes before kicking.
- Spin as fast as possible to increase your power and stability. Add a jump while extending the kick to do so even further.

Training Exercise: Slow kicks for technique and strength.
1. Stand facing a wall with your palms flat against it at shoulder height. Lift your knee up in a chamber position as high as possible, between your body and the wall, while keeping your palms pressed flat.
2. Slowly deliver the kick moving beneath your body without removing either of your hands. This will ensure you do not lean too far forward and that your kick is coming fully beneath the body.
3. Look at the heel. Hold the leg out at full extension for five seconds, focus on utilizing your back and glutes to maintain the position, then slowly return to the chamber.
4. Repeat the kicks five to ten times on each leg. Increase the time holding the kick extended to make it more challenging.

Success Story

The story of what is often considered one of the greatest knockout kicks in the history of the UFC (Ultimate Fighting Championship) belongs to American fighter Joaquin Buckley.

While jumping back kicks are usually successful in combat sports like taekwondo and sport karate, it is rare to see them used effectively in MMA; however, under the right circumstances, they are incredible.

In a bout between Joaquin Buckley and Impa Kasanganay in 2020, the fight immediately started out as a brawl with both men landing punches, kicks, and takedowns in what appeared to be a close matchup. The first time Buckley threw a roundhouse kick and Kasanganay caught it, the kicker managed to escape and returned to stand-up fighting. The defining moment, however, came when the action was repeated in the second round.

Buckley threw a roundhouse, and it was caught again. Then, demonstrating exceptional creativity and athleticism, which the fighter himself said comes from growing up watching martial arts movies, he launched into a spinning jump, freeing his captured leg and throwing his heel into Kasanganay's face with a perfectly executed jumping back kick.

This extraordinary move resulted in one of the greatest combat sport knockouts of all time, abruptly ending the bout in favor of Buckley. Subsequently, the kick was viewed more than sixty-five million times online and commented on publicly by everyone from the then-president Trump to musician Kanye West, turning Buckley from a young fighter struggling to make a mark into an overnight celebrity.

CHAPTER TWO

Circular Kicks

The kicks covered in this chapter are defined by their circular angle of attack, travelling in a horizontal motion around the fighter toward the opponent.

While straight kicks are faster and more direct, circular kicks offer a different approach toward striking. The force that can be developed from rotation using the back, abs, core, and hips is not only extremely powerful but also intuitive. Circular kicks can also easily be adapted for different heights and targets with relative ease.

These interchangeable angles of attack can be used to surprise opponents and provide much-needed variation in a fighter's arsenal. This is crucial in both competitive and real-life situations, as with each repetition of a particular kick (or a similar one), the likelihood of it being blocked or avoided increases exponentially.

This chapter will feature different types of roundhouse kicks, which are the "bread and butter" of most combat sports, and the hook kick, which is inherently difficult to use but will undoubtedly serve as "highlight reel" strike if landed effectively.

Roundhouse Snap Kick

The roundhouse snap kick is an extremely fast technique that can be thrown from either the lead or rear leg. However, in most situations it is best used as a speed strike from the lead leg.

The kick is extremely effective for disrupting an opponent's rhythm or controlling range when thrown at lower targets. It is also effective when used offensively as part of a combination of strikes, aiming at the torso or head to finish a fight. However, in high-kicking situations, it has the potential disadvantage of leaving the fighter off balance.

Power is generated using a release of the hip muscles and quadriceps coupled with the momentum of a rotation on the standing foot and a snap of the knee.

Character: This kick is like a jab punch, using an explosive whipping motion with a fast recoil that usually serves to stun an opponent rather than knock them clean out. Although when landed just right or included as part of a combination, it does have that capability.

Striking Surface: Traditionally, this kick uses the ball of the foot with the toes pulled back as the striking surface. However, in the modern day, it is more commonly used with the instep, which requires less foot flexibility and precision to be effective.

Targets: Side of the knee, thigh, floating ribs, neck, jaw, temple.

Common in: Karate, taekwondo, MMA, kickboxing.

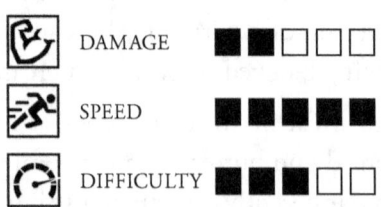

DAMAGE ■■□□□
SPEED ■■■■■
DIFFICULTY ■■■□□

Procedure

1. From a fighting stance, turn the rear foot out at 45 degrees so the toes point away from the target (thus allowing you to open the hips). Do this just as you begin to kick.

2. Raise your lead leg into a chamber so it is pointing slightly past your opponent to ensure you are kicking "through" rather than "against" the target. The sharper the angle of the chamber, the higher the kick.

3. Extend the foot in a straight line, straightening up the body to align the shoulder, hip, and heel. At the same time, continue to turn the standing foot 180-degrees away from the target, enabling the hips to open fully.

4. Re-chamber the lead leg and immediately step down in front, without leaning your body weight forward.

Possible Setup

1. As your opponent pushes forward, shift your body weight backward, throwing a defensive jab.

2. If they continue to push forward, step your lead leg back, opening the hips, and throw a jab with your new lead hand to keep them away.

3. Immediately after, roundhouse snap kick from the lead leg to the groin, thigh, knee, or calf, disrupting the opponent's momentum and giving you space to follow up.

Kicking Tips
- Consider this kick like a jab, designed to shock and sting or create space by focusing on speed over strength.
- Throw your lead arm downward across the body to increase the power from your core.
- Ensure your standing foot turns a full 180 degrees to release the full power of your hips.
- Pull your striking leg back to the chamber as fast as you kick or even faster to ensure maximum power.

Training Exercise: Low-middle-high combos (for technique and accuracy).

a) Either holding onto the back of a chair or standing on the rear leg, chamber the front leg at medium height and deliver a low kick (leg level).
b) Without stepping down or lowering the chamber, deliver the same kick at chest level, then head level.
c) Change legs and follow the same procedure.
d) Complete this drill three times, at slow, medium, and full speeds.

Success Story

A former training partner of mine was a karate world champion but his regular job was in construction. After one particularly long day at work, he stopped by a local shop to pick up something for his dinner, still in his high-visibility jacket and steel-toed boots.

As he was selecting his meal, there was shouting from the front of the store. The martial artist peered around the aisle to see a young guy, hood pulled up over his face, screaming in the face of the shopkeeper, demanding the older woman hand over her day's earnings. To make matters worse, he was brandishing a ball-peen hammer, waving it aggressively in her face and smacking it on the counter.

The martial artist, enraged by injustice, forgot his meal and instead trod quietly along the aisle toward the counter. As the shopkeeper pulled a wad of cash out, the robber snatched it greedily and turned to make his escape. Instead of seeing freedom, he saw a size-forty-four steel-toed boot whipping up from the ground and cracking him around the temple. Obviously, it was lights out.

The police were called, and the martial artist was taken into custody while they figured out what had happened. After a half hour of waiting, a uniformed officer came into the holding room, grinning. He shook the kicker's hand and told him that the CCTV footage was the most badass thing he had ever seen and that he was free to go.

Having been kicked in the face by the guy a bunch of times myself, I have no doubts about the veracity of the story. However, it should be noted that this was only possible due to his incredible level of training and skill. For the rest of us, especially in self-defense situations against armed opponents, high kicks pose a huge risk and should NOT be attempted. Similarly, actively getting involved with violence always carries legal risks and, in this case, the kicker was lucky to have got away without any criminal charges!

Roundhouse Slam Kick

This version of the roundhouse is common in muay thai and Southeast Asian kickboxing styles, as well as most full-contact kicking sports. It is hard to block as it often comes straight from the floor and doesn't need a high chamber like many other kicks. Fighters usually throw it from the rear leg, with a quick switch of the feet preceding the kick if required.

This kick is often used offensively toward the middle and high section, either to stun the opponent or cause serious damage and end the fight. However, it can also be used on low targets as a defensive tool to control space, open an opponent to an attack, or wear them down and stifle their ability to move properly.

Rotation from the rear foot, the release of the hips, and a swing of the leg utilizing the back and torso muscles power the kick. This motion, rather than an extension of the knee, makes it slower but more powerful and easier to deliver than its snapping equivalent.

Character: As the name suggests, the character of this kick is a slamming motion that drives through the target like a swinging baseball bat. This motion is easy to see when fighters miss the kick and must turn the entire way through 360 degrees to release the power generated.

Striking Surface: The foot or shin, depending on range. While this gives variation over distance, it also means that the bones need to be well-conditioned to withstand the force of the blow.

Targets: Calf, thigh, ribs, side of head.

Common in: Various kickboxing styles, MMA, sanda.

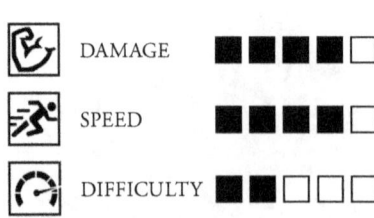

Procedure

1. Begin standing loosely with the weight mostly on the rear leg and shoulders almost square to your opponent. Step your lead foot out at a 45-degree angle and shift your weight forward onto the ball of your lead foot.

2. Lift the striking leg into a chamber close to hip height, with your knee angled toward your target (a steeper angle to kick higher, a lower angle to kick lower).

3. Rise up onto the ball of your foot and thrust the kicking leg out. Continue to turn your standing foot away and throw your lead arm downward as the kick reaches full extension.

4. Quickly pull this leg back to its starting position traveling from the same path, keeping your hands raised, ready to attack.

Possible Setup

1. Throw a jab, skipping forward, and raise the front knee as though you are going to do a front snap kick, making sure you keep your face covered by your hand and your weight back.

2. As your opponent recoils or goes to block, shoot the standing leg outside of his body at 45 degrees.

3. Immediately afterward, throw a low roundhouse with the shin into the opponent's abdomen or rear thigh.

Kicking Tips
- Always work the kick in a flow of attacks, and try to minimize the time between punches and the roundhouse until it is almost non-existent.
- Ensure you keep your momentum travelling through the strike by staying on the ball of the foot and turning the body while opening your hips fully.
- As this kick is mostly thrown from the rear leg and uses a significant wind-up, work on changing legs quickly from the front to the rear. Do this by adding a small skip to switch their position.

Training Exercise: Speed kicks for accuracy, power, and ferocity.
1. With a partner holding pads at leg or torso height, try to deliver as many kicks as possible in bursts of consecutive kicks lasting five to ten seconds.
2. Speed and aggression are the name of the game in this drill, so ensure your partner shifts his or her weight to absorb the impact of each kick.
3. Make it more difficult by having your partner move in and out and change sides randomly so you must adjust for distance and switch feet depending on their position.

Hook Kick

The hook kick involves swinging the leg out horizontally away from the target, then whipping the foot back in a hooking motion that ideally uses the heel to make impact. It is far faster to perform using the front leg, so this is typically preferred.

It can be delivered to the front side of an opponent facing you in a mirrored stance, aiming at the groin, abdomen, or face. It can also be used as a counter to slip past an opponent and attack the rear side of his body. This uses the heel to kick the spine, legs, or the back of the head.

A combination of the back and hip muscles retracting in unison generates most of the power for this kick through a whipping backward motion.

Character: The hook kick features a snatching motion. It is similar to the lash of a whip as it hits a vertical pole or pillar and wraps around it, or to the weighted ball at the end of a morningstar or flail.

Striking Surface: Ideally the heel, which serves as a weight at the end of the whip and lands hard. In sporting contexts, the flat or ball of the foot is often used to increase reach but drastically reduces damage.

Targets: Chest, face, or abdomen (front side). Knees, kidneys, spine, back of head (back side).

Common in: Taekwondo, karate, kung fu.

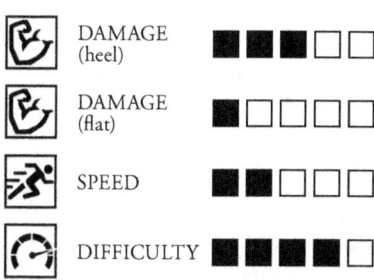

Procedure

1. From your normal fighting stance, step the lead leg out at approximately 30 degrees, about one foot out past the opponent's lead leg, while keeping your eyes forward to avoid telegraphing the kick.

2. Lift the lead leg up in front of the body with the knee high and tight to the chest, and reach your lead hand out, preparing to swing forward to give you momentum.

3. Straighten the kicking leg, at an angle away from the body, turning the rear foot away. Extend the heel and lean slightly backward, reaching the arm down.

4. Whip the heel back, throw the lead arm forward, lining up the heel, hip, shoulders, and arm at the moment of contact. Continue to pull the strike through and step down in front onto the lead leg.

Possible Setup

1. Keep the lead arm down, inviting the opponent to jab. As they do, slide backward, leaning your weight away and turning the rear foot.

2. From this position chamber the foot at a 45-degree angle from your opponent's body.

3. Whip the heel back into the opponent's abdomen, groin, or even lead leg to use it as a sweep.

Kicking Tips:
- Ensure your kicking foot goes out past the center of your body, otherwise the kick will not land, or it will be extremely weak.
- Extend the kick beyond your back at the final position to ensure the back muscles are engaged. Add more of a backward tilt to increase the angle.
- For alternative versions, use the hook to the lead leg of your opponent as a sweep or spin away from them to kick with the rear leg.

Training Exercise: Slow hooks for accuracy and flexibility.
1. Hold onto the back of a chair for balance (you can remove this later once you've built up strength and balance) and raise the chamber up to kicking height.
2. Practice slowly extending the leg fully away from the target and slowly hooking backward, extending as far through as possible.
3. Perform five to ten repetitions on each side.
4. Increase the height and downward angle of your head and body to make the exercise more challenging.

Success Story

In the 2004 Summer Olympic Games, a matchup took place that was so perfect it could almost have been lifted straight from a Hollywood movie.

The games were being held in Greece. Fighting for gold in the men's heavyweight division of taekwondo was a Greek fighter, Alexandros Nikolaidis, who towered over his opponent at six feet seven inches. Nikolaidis was a firm fan favorite, vying to take home the nation's first gold in this category before an audience of his countrymen. His opponent, representing South Korea—the ancestral homeland of taekwondo—was Moon Dae-Sung. He was shorter, lighter, and fighting on the other man's turf, but he had a legacy to secure: that of Korean domination of their sport against taller, stronger foreign fighters.

As the fighters met in the center of the ring, the Greek started throwing spin kicks and axe kicks, using his vast reach and flexibility to control the distance. Meanwhile, Moon was left to dodge and counter, wary of getting close enough, but he managed to score the first clean hit with a roundhouse kick to Nikolaidis's torso.

The two men, both hesitant to commit, stared each other down, waiting for the other to make the first move. Nikolaidis, feeling confident, launched forward with a front-leg roundhouse snap kick, trying to even the score. As he kicked, Moon spun out of range, jumping and turning with a rear leg kick that slammed into Nikolaidis' head, knocking him clean out. This was one of the most visually stunning and significant kicks ever landed in the Olympic Games.

CHAPTER THREE

Unusual-Angle Kicks

This chapter will look at the unorthodox kicks that strike using uncommon angles of attack. Although less uniform than previous chapters in this book, the kicks presented here are all extremely useful as they can (and often do) catch opponents off guard. They are particularly useful against those who are used to fighting within a particular rule set or methodology.

Because of their unusual angles of attack, the techniques in this section offer fighters versatility, allowing them to deliver kicks when in areas with obstacles or limited space.

While these unusual-angle kicks are not always as powerful or intuitive as their straight or circular counterparts, they are valuable tools to be added to one's arsenal.

The kicks in this final chapter include the question mark kick (a version of the roundhouse slam kick) that uses a curving, downward trajectory; the oblique kick that comes at a downward angle toward the low section; and up kicks, which launch straight from the floor near vertically upward.

Question Mark Kick

This is an unorthodox approach to the roundhouse slam kick. It begins by raising the leg as though to deliver a front or oblique kick, then at the last moment twisting from the hip outward, bringing the foot around in a question mark circular shape, either over the top of the opponent's guard to kick the head or below the guard to target the ribs or legs.

Many professional combat sport fighters and those in self-defense situations use it to great effect, primarily because of its deceptive nature. While the question mark kick can be performed with the rear leg as a power strike, this usually requires a good fake to make it surprising. Therefore, it is easier to throw quickly from the lead leg.

The kick is typically offensive and makes the opponent go to block a low kick before sneakily sliding in over the top, delivering a powerful strike to the head or other targets while it is left unguarded.

The question mark kick generates power by turning outward, then reverses the direction, quickly shifting on the standing leg. Meanwhile, the foot follows with a whipping motion. This power is extended by a downward pull from the lead hip and a thrust from the quadriceps.

Character: This kick should feel like a snake attack. It travels upward in a wave, like a serpent's body releasing from a coil. It then explodes downward into the target with a stinging bite.

Striking Surface: Typically the top of the foot or lower shin when in close range.

Targets: Side of head, neck, clavicle.

Common in: Muay thai, Khmer boxing, MMA, kickboxing.

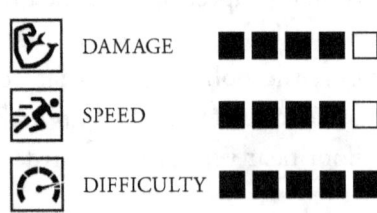

Procedure

1. Shift the weight back onto the rear leg and raise the lead knee into a horizontal chamber as if delivering a front snap kick, but with the toes pointed downward.

2. Pull the hip quickly sideways into a horizontal chamber as though delivering a snapping roundhouse. Turn the torso 90 degrees and the standing foot 180 degrees away from the opponent.

3. Rotate the torso even further away from the target, extending the kicking foot and turning your lead hip until it is pointing towards the ground. The kick is now travelling in a downward trajectory.

4. Quickly lift the foot back and re-chamber so it does not get stuck on the opponent's clavicle or in the crook of their arm and step down in front.

Possible Setup

1. Deliver an oblique kick (see the next section) or check the opponent's knee, then throw a cross to push them backward.

2. Continue to move forward, raising the lead leg, making the opponent expect another check or oblique kick.

3. Immediately whip the hip sideways, reversing the direction, throwing the low question mark kick into their thigh or the back of the knee.

Kicking Tips
- Ensure you spin the hip and body fully, rotating on the standing foot as though delivering a roundhouse while turning the kicking hip all the way toward the floor.
- Focus on speed over power. The whipping motion of this kick when thrown fast will easily do enough damage that you do not need to muscle through it.
- When you have the basic action down, reduce the extension of the knee raise or try to deliver it from a fake front or oblique kick position.

Training Exercise: Heavy bag feints and kicks for speed and setups
1. Practice on a heavy bag while holding a pad facing downward between you and the bag at shoulder height. Deliver a light knee to the pad (without leaning over).
2. Quickly re-chamber and throw the question mark kick to the bag at head or neck height.
3. Add complexity by putting a stool or chair at your side, approximately 45-degrees between you and the bag. This will ensure you need to re-chamber fully before kicking to make it over the obstacle.

Oblique Kick

The oblique kick uses the arch of the foot in a stomping or swinging motion to attack the opponent's leg or to check an incoming kick. Although usually not completely prohibited in combat sports, many consider the oblique kick to be unsportsmanlike. It is also a staple of self-defense systems due to this effectiveness and simple delivery.

In traditional martial arts and self-defense systems, the oblique kick is usually coupled with a stomping motion and can be delivered to either the inner or outer side of the knee (often causing long-lasting injury). However, it can also be used as a defensive move to stop an approaching opponent by landing on the hip, or to check incoming kicks by hitting the thigh or shin.

The power of the oblique kick comes from a stomping or swinging motion (depending on the target), driving downward from the hips and quads coupled with gravity.

Character: The oblique kick has the feeling of a downward plunge, like a shovel being lifted and thrust down into the dirt, or in this case the foot into the opponent's legs.

Striking Surface: The arch of the foot or heel.

Targets: Hip, thigh, knee, shin, ankle, foot.

Common in: Wing chun, white crane, karate, savate, krav maga, MMA, self-defense systems.

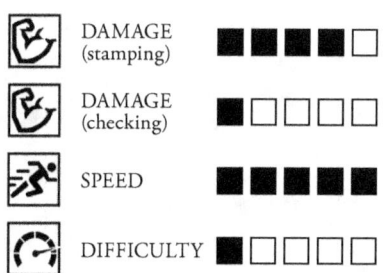

	DAMAGE (stamping)	■■■■□
	DAMAGE (checking)	■□□□□
	SPEED	■■■■■
	DIFFICULTY	■□□□□

Procedure

1. With both hands raised, step the lead leg out across the body to ensure you are almost square, facing the opponent.

2. Lift the rear knee up from the floor to just above waist height while keeping the weight mostly on the standing leg.

3. Thrust down from the hip, angling the instep into the thigh or shin from a straight position, or the knee if you are to either side of the target. Use more of a swinging motion to check a kick.

4. Withdraw the leg, coming back up to a chamber and step out (left) or step through, crushing the knee (right).

Possible Setup

1. Launch an open-handed technique toward the opponent's face as a distraction, keeping eye contact. This obscures their vision and keeps their attention high.

2. Step up with the front leg and lean slightly back on impact to stay out of range.

3. Thrust down, stomping into the knee and drive it into the ground.

Kicking Tips
- Ensure you do not rise up on your standing leg before kicking. This will make it easier to see and easier for you to lose balance.
- Do not fall forward with your head coming downward as you land, or you will be easily exposed to counterattacks.
- Practice chambering lower and adding more of a swing to the leg to inflict less damage or check an opponent's kick.

Training Exercise: Resistance band stomps.
1. Hold a resistance band in one hand and hook it under the heel.
2. Keeping the hands raised, push down, using the leg and core muscles and ensuring you turn the foot all the way out and reach maximum extension.
3. Repeat for ten to fifteen repetitions on each leg, working on speed and power as you get more comfortable with the movement.
4. Increase the difficulty by using a stronger resistance band or by adding a kicking pad which is face up, leaned diagonally against a wall.

Success Story

I was at a friend's birthday party where I lived in downtown Hanoi, Vietnam. We'd had a few drinks and ended up at a sketchy (allegedly) Mafia-run bar down on the banks of the Red River. The view was great, looking over a patch of banana trees down onto the muddy plains of the river that local legend claims are still dotted with unexploded landmines from the Vietnam War period. The club had two outside areas connected by only a narrow concrete path that dropped off ten feet into a muddy grove below.

Some friends were laughing and joking a little raucously when they attracted the attention of a group of local young men who looked like they didn't take too kindly to the intrusion. There were a few shouted exchanges, then people started springing to their feet. I moved between the two groups, hoping to act as a mediator and preferring to talk my way out of trouble rather than rely on force. But one of the local boys, obviously drunk, moved toward us, his body language screaming that he was going to take a swing at someone.

As I stepped within range, I thrust my foot out, the arch nestling into his hip, catching him exactly as he stepped. The guy's weight folded backward and he fell into his friends, conveniently blocking the path between the two groups. After that, my friends made a quick exit, diving through the doors into the club to be instantly lost among the sea of bodies, deafening techno, and flashing lights.

Luckily, my decision hadn't inflicted any serious damage. Even more importantly, he'd simply fallen back into his buddies rather than tumbled off the edge of the path down into no man's land. This was, in my opinion, the best kind of self-defense—where no one suffers any lasting consequences.

Up Kick

Up kicks are one of the staple ground-fighting techniques of modern combat sports. They are equally useful in self-defense situations where the defender has fallen, slipped, or is facing multiple attackers. They are delivered from the floor, with the kicker lying on their back facing a standing opponent and thrusting the heels upward.

Often thrown in combinations using both legs, up kicks are primarily defensive, aimed at stopping the standing opponent from inflicting any further damage, or making space for you to return to your feet. They can be used against the face, body, or legs to push, strike, hook, or all of the above mixed together. While up kicks rarely finish fights, they do have the potential to do so but must be timed perfectly to cause significant damage.

Power is generated by throwing your hips upward and pushing off the ground with your back at the same time as you thrust your feet up into the face or stomach of the opponent.

Character: Up kicks should feel like you are stabbing aggressively upward at someone overhead with a spear or staff as they make the mistake of getting close enough to you.

Striking Surface: The flat of the foot or heel is used to thrust upward in combinations.

Targets: Knee, groin, abdomen, chest, face.

Common in: Self-defense systems, MMA.

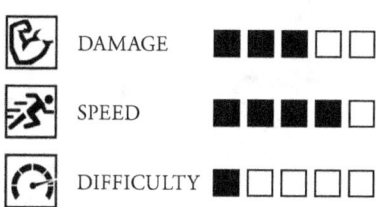

Procedure

1. Lie on your back with the soles of the feet facing your opponent and with your hands raised defensively, knees tucked up to your chest and your head and shoulders raised up as much as possible.

2. Keep one foot extended, ideally pressed against your opponent to control space. Maneuver using your legs or back to keep your feet pointed at your opponent as they try to circle around or attack you.

3. Use your core and thigh muscles to explode, straightening the leg and projecting the heels or a flat foot upward. Repeat with the opposite foot in combinations of two to three kicks, creating space to stand up.

4. Use one hand and one foot on the ground to slide out of range and quickly step back up onto your feet without turning your back or lowering your guard.

Possible Setup

1. After falling backward, lower your hands and feet to tempt your attacker(s) into coming at you and trying to take advantage of the situation.

2. As they close distance, tuck up tightly and explode upward from the ground, covering your head and kicking viciously.

3. When they back off stunned, return to your feet without turning away and prepare to attack.

Kicking Tips
- Always stay on your back and do not turn onto your side or knees, as you will be at risk of attack from behind.
- Use up kicks in explosive combinations of one, two, or more. Try pushing one foot against the knee or shin of the attacker or hooking it around their leg to help keep your feet aimed at them.
- Never turn your back when standing up or you will be open to critical damage.

Training Exercise: Escape the gauntlet for self-defense practice.
1. Have a training partner (or partners) circle you with one hand holding a pad at abdomen height.
2. They must maneuver around you, trying to get close enough to touch your head.
3. You must kick them away and turn to face the next attack (or attackers) until you create enough space to stand up.
4. Start slowly and increase speed and pressure until it is impossible to keep them away from you any longer.

AFTERWORD

I hope you have found some useful techniques, training drills, and advice in this book.

To reiterate the advice in the introduction of this book, it is not recommended that every reader master each variant of all the kicks in this book. If you are able to use even half of these kicks with some level of proficiency, you will be well on your way to developing an effective arsenal of techniques that can be applied in traditional martial arts settings, competition, or self-defense.

It is also recommended that fighters do not focus only on certain aspects of their practice in martial arts and combat sports training (although we do, of course, all have our own favorites, strengths, and weaknesses). Regarding kicking, this is particularly important as it is tempting to focus only on your stronger or more flexible side.

Personally, I believe that in order to keep progressing, fighters must develop the areas in which they are weakest, as this will allow them to become fully rounded and capable in combat.

As a result of the above, I thoroughly advocate cross training in a variety of martial arts or combat sports since I truly believe that every style or system has something to offer for anyone serious about developing their skills.

In order to become a well-rounded martial artist, it is also recommended that fighters include a variety of punches and open-hand strikes, knees and elbows, locks and chokes, and throws and sweeps into their repertoire of functional techniques. I intend to cover each of the aforementioned areas in subsequent books.

Finally, if you enjoyed this book, please remember to leave a review online wherever you bought it, or recommend it to a friend, training partner, or colleague. Meanwhile, if you have any questions or comments regarding the content of this book or the author, please reach out directly via my website www.augustusjohnroe.com. I am always happy to hear from you!

Many thanks and happy training!

Acknowledgements

As with any book, this has been a collaborative effort. For their help with writing, photography, design, and editing this book I would like to thank Thanh Ha, Clement Martin, Le Duc Anh, and Jasper Roe.

I would also like to thank the contributors of the "Success Stories" I have used, both public figures and those who allowed me to share their tales.

GLOSSARY OF TERMS

Abs: Short for abdominal muscles. They support your spine, assist in trunk movement, and play a vital role in maintaining posture and stability.

Backfist: A strike either vertically or horizontally that uses the back of the fist and top of the knuckles as a striking surface.

Chamber: The defensive or pre-kicking position, where the foot is raised but the leg has not yet been extended.

Cross: A powerful straight punch that comes across the body, usually following a jab.

Glutes: The glutes are the muscles in your buttocks that help with movements like hip extension, rotation, and abduction.

Guard: The defensive position where a fighter has both hands raised to protect the head (or one to protect the head and another to protect the body).

Jab: A quick, lead-hand punch designed to shock, create openings, or stun an opponent.

Oblique (Muscles): The series of muscles that run along either side of the rib cage and enable you to twist and bend side to side by contracting the abdomen.

Oblique Kick: A kick that comes from a slanting, non-parallel position.

PNF: Proprioceptive neuromuscular facilitation is a stretching method that relies on a series of contraction and relaxation to increase flexibility within a muscle.

Quads: Quadriceps—the muscles at the front of your thigh crucial for activities like walking, running, and jumping.

Uppercut: A punch thrown with the lead hand at an upward angle from the body, usually catching the opponent under the chin.

ABOUT THE AUTHOR

Augustus John Roe is an author, linguist, and instructor of martial arts, including traditional styles, combat sports, and self-defense and weapon systems. For more than a decade, he has lived and trained in Asia. During this time, Augustus has worked on numerous television shows, books, magazines, and academic projects documenting local cultures and martial-arts practices.

For more information about any of his work, including upcoming nonfiction works and blog posts, please follow him on social media and visit his website: www.augustusjohnroe.com

BOOKS FROM YMAA

- 101 REFLECTIONS ON TAI CHI CHUAN
- 108 INSIGHTS INTO TAI CHI CHUAN
- A WOMAN'S QIGONG GUIDE
- ADVANCING IN TAE KWON DO
- ANALYSIS OF GENUINE KARATE
- ANALYSIS OF GENUINE KARATE 2
- ANALYSIS OF SHU HA RI IN KARATE-DO
- ANALYSIS OF SHAOLIN CHIN NA 2ND ED
- ANCIENT CHINESE WEAPONS
- ART AND SCIENCE OF STAFF FIGHTING
- THE ART AND SCIENCE OF SELF-DEFENSE
- ART AND SCIENCE OF STICK FIGHTING
- ART OF HOJO UNDO
- ARTHRITIS RELIEF
- BACK PAIN RELIEF
- BAGUAZHANG
- BRAIN FITNESS
- CHIN NA IN GROUND FIGHTING
- CHINESE FAST WRESTLING
- CHINESE FITNESS
- CHINESE TUI NA MASSAGE
- COMPLETE MARTIAL ARTIST
- COMPREHENSIVE APPLICATIONS OF SHAOLIN CHIN NA
- CONFLICT COMMUNICATION
- DAO DE JING: A QIGONG INTERPRETATION
- DAO IN ACTION
- DEFENSIVE TACTICS
- DIRTY GROUND
- DR. WU'S HEAD MASSAGE
- ESSENCE OF SHAOLIN WHITE CRANE
- EXPLORING TAI CHI
- FACING VIOLENCE
- FIGHT LIKE A PHYSICIST
- THE FIGHTER'S BODY
- FIGHTER'S FACT BOOK 1&2
- FIGHTING THE PAIN RESISTANT ATTACKER
- FIRST DEFENSE
- FORCE DECISIONS: A CITIZENS GUIDE
- HOMECOMING SERIES
- INSIDE TAI CHI
- JUDO ADVANTAGE
- JUJI GATAME ENCYCLOPEDIA
- KARATE SCIENCE
- KEPPAN
- KRAV MAGA COMBATIVES
- KRAV MAGA FUNDAMENTAL STRATEGIES
- KRAV MAGA PROFESSIONAL TACTICS
- KRAV MAGA WEAPON DEFENSES
- LITTLE BLACK BOOK OF VIOLENCE
- LIUHEBAFA FIVE CHARACTER SECRETS
- MARTIAL ARTS OF VIETNAM
- MARTIAL ARTS INSTRUCTION
- MARTIAL WAY AND ITS VIRTUES
- MEDITATIONS ON VIOLENCE
- MERIDIAN QIGONG EXERCISES
- MINDFUL EXERCISE
- MIND INSIDE TAI CHI
- MIND INSIDE YANG STYLE TAI CHI CHUAN
- NORTHERN SHAOLIN SWORD
- OKINAWA'S COMPLETE KARATE SYSTEM: ISSHIN RYU
- PRINCIPLES OF TRADITIONAL CHINESE MEDICINE
- PROTECTOR ETHIC
- QIGONG FOR HEALTH & MARTIAL ARTS
- QIGONG FOR TREATING COMMON AILMENTS
- QIGONG MASSAGE
- QIGONG MEDITATION: EMBRYONIC BREATHING
- QIGONG GRAND CIRCULATION
- QIGONG MEDITATION: SMALL CIRCULATION
- QIGONG, THE SECRET OF YOUTH: DA MO'S CLASSICS
- ROOT OF CHINESE QIGONG
- SAFEST FAMILY ON THE BLOCK
- SAMBO ENCYCLOPEDIA
- SCALING FORCE
- SELF-DEFENSE FOR WOMEN
- SHIN GI TAI: KARATE TRAINING
- SIMPLE CHINESE MEDICINE
- SIMPLE QIGONG EXERCISES FOR HEALTH, 3RD ED.
- SIMPLIFIED TAI CHI CHUAN, 2ND ED.
- SOLO TRAINING 1&2
- SPOTTING DANGER BEFORE IT SPOTS YOU
- SPOTTING DANGER BEFORE IT SPOTS YOUR KIDS
- SPOTTING DANGER BEFORE IT SPOTS YOUR TEENS
- SPOTTING DANGER FOR TRAVELERS
- SUMO FOR MIXED MARTIAL ARTS
- SUNRISE TAI CHI
- SURVIVING ARMED ASSAULTS
- TAE KWON DO: THE KOREAN MARTIAL ART
- TAEKWONDO BLACK BELT POOMSAE
- TAEKWONDO: A PATH TO EXCELLENCE
- TAEKWONDO: ANCIENT WISDOM
- TAEKWONDO: DEFENSE AGAINST WEAPONS
- TAEKWONDO: SPIRIT AND PRACTICE
- TAI CHI BALL QIGONG: FOR HEALTH AND MARTIAL ARTS
- TAI CHI BALL QIGONG
- THE TAI CHI BOOK
- TAI CHI CHIN NA
- TAI CHI CHUAN CLASSICAL YANG STYLE
- TAI CHI CHUAN MARTIAL APPLICATIONS
- TAI CHI CHUAN MARTIAL POWER
- TAI CHI CONCEPTS AND EXPERIMENTS
- TAI CHI DYNAMICS
- TAI CHI FOR DEPRESSION
- TAI CHI IN 10 WEEKS
- TAI CHI PUSH HANDS
- TAI CHI QIGONG
- TAI CHI SECRETS OF THE ANCIENT MASTERS
- TAI CHI SECRETS OF THE WU & LI STYLES
- TAI CHI SECRETS OF THE WU STYLE
- TAI CHI SECRETS OF THE YANG STYLE
- TAI CHI SWORD: CLASSICAL YANG STYLE
- TAI CHI SWORD FOR BEGINNERS
- TAI CHI WALKING
- TAI CHI CHUAN THEORY OF DR. YANG, JWING-MING
- TOP 10 KICKS FIGHTING ARTS
- TRADITIONAL CHINESE HEALTH SECRETS TRADITIONAL TAEKWONDO
- TRAINING FOR SUDDEN VIOLENCE
- TRIANGLE HOLD ENCYCLOPEDIA
- TRUE WELLNESS SERIES (MIND, HEART, GUT) WARRIOR'S MANIFESTO
- WAY OF KATA
- WAY OF SANCHIN KATA
- WAY TO BLACK BELT
- WESTERN HERBS FOR MARTIAL ARTISTS
- WILD GOOSE QIGONG
- WING CHUN IN-DEPTH
- WINNING FIGHTS
- XINGYIQUAN

AND MANY MORE . . .

VIDEOS FROM YMAA

- ANALYSIS OF SHAOLIN CHIN NA
- ART AND SCIENCE OF SELF DEFENSE
- ART AND SCIENCE OF STAFF FIGHTING
- ART AND SCIENCE STICK FIGHTING
- ART AND SCIENCE SWORD FIGHTING
- BAGUA FOR BEGINNERS 1 & 2
- BEGINNER QIGONG FOR WOMEN 1 & 2
- BEGINNER TAI CHI FOR HEALTH
- BREATH MEDICINE
- BIOENERGY TRAINING 1&2
- CHEN TAI CHI CANNON FIST
- CHEN TAI CHI FIRST FORM
- CHEN TAI CHI FOR BEGINNERS
- CHIN NA IN-DEPTH SERIES
- FACING VIOLENCE: 7 THINGS A MARTIAL ARTIST MUST KNOW
- FIVE ANIMAL SPORTS
- FIVE ELEMENTS ENERGY BALANCE
- HEALER WITHIN: MEDICAL QIGONG
- INFIGHTING
- INTRODUCTION TO QI GONG FOR BEGINNERS
- JOINT LOCKS
- KUNG FU BODY CONDITIONING 1 & 2
- KUNG FU FOR KIDS AND TEENS SERIES
- MERIDIAN QIGONG
- NEIGONG FOR MARTIAL ARTS
- NORTHERN SHAOLIN SWORD
- QI GONG 30-DAY CHALLENGE
- QI GONG FOR ANXIETY
- QI GONG FOR ARMS, WRISTS, AND HANDS
- QIGONG FOR BEGINNERS: FRAGRANCE
- QI GONG FOR BETTER BALANCE
- QI GONG FOR BETTER BREATHING
- QI GONG FOR CANCER
- QI GONG FOR DEPRESSION
- QI GONG FOR ENERGY AND VITALITY
- QI GONG FOR HEADACHES
- QIGONG FOR HEALTH: BETTER DIGESTION
- QIGONG FOR HEALTH: HEALING QIGONG EXERCISES
- QIGONG FOR HEALTH: IMMUNE SYSTEM
- QIGONG FOR HEALTH: JOINT REHABILITATION
- QIGONG FOR HEALTH: MERIDIAN EXTREMITIES
- QIGONG FOR HEALTH: SITTING QIGONG EXERCISES
- QIGONG FOR HEALTH: SPINE AND BACK
- QI GONG FOR THE HEALTHY HEART
- QI GONG FOR HEALTHY JOINTS
- QI GONG FOR HIGH BLOOD PRESSURE
- QIGONG FOR LONGEVITY
- QI GONG FOR STRONG BONES
- QI GONG FOR THE UPPER BACK AND NECK
- QIGONG FOR WOMEN WITH DAISY LEE
- QIGONG FLOW FOR STRESS & ANXIETY RELIEF
- QIGONG GRAND CIRCULATION
- QIGONG MASSAGE
- QIGONG MINDFULNESS IN MOTION
- QI GONG—THE SEATED WORKOUT
- QIGONG: 15 MINUTES TO HEALTH
- SABER FUNDAMENTAL TRAINING
- SAI TRAINING AND SEQUENCES
- SANCHIN KATA: TRADITIONAL TRAINING FOR KARATE POWER
- SCALING FORCE
- SEARCHING FOR SUPERHUMANS
- SHAOLIN KUNG FU FUNDAMENTAL TRAINING: COURSES 1 & 2
- SHAOLIN LONG FIST KUNG FU BEGINNER-INTERMEDIATE-ADVANCED SERIES
- SHAOLIN SABER: BASIC SEQUENCES
- SHAOLIN STAFF: BASIC SEQUENCES
- SHAOLIN WHITE CRANE GONG FU BASIC TRAINING SERIES
- SHUAI JIAO: KUNG FU WRESTLING
- SIMPLE QIGONG EXERCISES FOR HEALTH
- SIMPLE QIGONG EXERCISES FOR ARTHRITIS RELIEF
- SIMPLE QIGONG EXERCISES FOR BACK PAIN RELIEF
- SIMPLIFIED TAI CHI CHUAN: 24 & 48 POSTURES
- SIMPLIFIED TAI CHI FOR BEGINNERS 48
- SPOTTING DANGER BEFORE IT SPOTS YOU
- SPOTTING DANGER FOR KIDS
- SPOTTING DANGER FOR TEENS
- SUN TAI CHI
- SWORD: FUNDAMENTAL TRAINING
- TAEKWONDO KORYO POOMSAE
- TAI CHI BALL QIGONG SERIES
- TAI CHI BALL WORKOUT FOR BEGINNERS
- TAI CHI CHUAN CLASSICAL YANG STYLE
- TAI CHI FIGHTING SET
- TAI CHI FIT: 24 FORM
- TAI CHI FIT: ALZHEIMER'S PREVENTION
- TAI CHI FIT: CANCER PREVENTION
- TAI CHI FIT FOR VETERANS
- TAI CHI FIT: FOR WOMEN
- TAI CHI FIT: FLOW
- TAI CHI FIT: FUSION BAMBOO
- TAI CHI FIT: FUSION FIRE
- TAI CHI FIT: FUSION IRON
- TAI CHI FIT: HEALTHY BACK SEATED WORKOUT
- TAI CHI FIT: HEALTHY HEART WORKOUT
- TAI CHI FIT IN PARADISE
- TAI CHI FIT: OVER 50
- TAI CHI FIT OVER 50: BALANCE EXERCISES
- TAI CHI FIT OVER 50: SEATED WORKOUT
- TAI CHI FIT OVER 60: GENTLE EXERCISES
- TAI CHI FIT OVER 60: HEALTHY JOINTS
- TAI CHI FIT OVER 60: LIVE LONGER
- TAI CHI FIT: STRENGTH
- TAI CHI FIT: TO GO
- TAI CHI FOR WOMEN
- TAI CHI FUSION: FIRE
- TAI CHI QIGONG
- TAI CHI PRINCIPLES FOR HEALTHY AGING
- TAI CHI PUSHING HANDS SERIES
- TAI CHI SWORD: CLASSICAL YANG STYLE
- TAI CHI SWORD FOR BEGINNERS
- TAI CHI SYMBOL: YIN YANG STICKING HANDS
- TAIJI & SHAOLIN STAFF: FUNDAMENTAL TRAINING
- TAIJI CHIN NA IN-DEPTH
- TAIJI 37 POSTURES MARTIAL APPLICATIONS
- TAIJI SABER CLASSICAL YANG STYLE
- TAIJI WRESTLING
- TRAINING FOR SUDDEN VIOLENCE
- UNDERSTANDING QIGONG SERIES
- WHITE CRANE HARD & SOFT QIGONG
- YANG TAI CHI FOR BEGINNERS
- YOQI: MICROCOSMIC ORBIT QIGONG
- YOQI QIGONG FOR A HAPPY HEART
- YOQI:QIGONG FLOW FOR HAPPY MIND
- YOQI:QIGONG FLOW FOR INTERNAL ALCHEMY
- YOQI QIGONG FOR HAPPY SPLEEN & STOMACH
- YOQI QIGONG FOR HAPPY KIDNEYS
- YOQI QIGONG FLOW FOR HAPPY LUNGS
- YOQI QIGONG FLOW FOR STRESS RELIEF
- YOQI: QIGONG FLOW TO BOOST IMMUNE SYSTEM
- YOQI SIX HEALING SOUNDS
- YOQI: YIN YOGA 1
- WU TAI CHI FOR BEGINNERS
- WUDANG KUNG FU: FUNDAMENTAL TRAINING
- WUDANG SWORD
- WUDANG TAIJIQUAN
- XINGYIQUAN
- YANG TAI CHI FOR BEGINNERS

AND MANY MORE . . .

more products available from . . .

YMAA Publication Center, Inc. 楊氏東方文化出版中心

1-800-669-8892 • info@ymaa.com • www.ymaa.com

www.ingramcontent.com/pod-product-compliance
Lightning Source LLC
Chambersburg PA
CBHW070148080526
44586CB00015B/1894